Bo and Zop
learn how to be an
EARTHLING

HOW DO EARTHLINGS LOOK AFTER THEIR PLANET?

by Kirsty Holmes

🌳 CRABTREE
PUBLISHING COMPANY

Author: Kirsty Holmes

Editorial director: Kathy Middleton

Editors: Madeline Tyler, Janine Deschenes

Proofreader: Melissa Boyce

Graphic design: Dan Scas

Production coordinator
& Prepress technician: Ken Wright

Print coordinator: Katherine Berti

Images

All images are courtesy of Shutterstock.com, unless otherwise specified.

Alien Bo: delcarmat. Alien Zop: Roi and Roi. Background – PremiumArt. Vectors throughout: kearia.

Speech bubbles: Surrphoto.

All facts, statistics, web addresses and URLs in this book were verified as valid and accurate at time of writing. No responsibility for any changes to external websites or references can be accepted by either the author or publisher.

Library and Achives Canada Cataloguing in Publication

Title: How do earthlings look after their planet? / Kirsty Holmes.
Other titles: Looking after your world
Names: Holmes, Kirsty, author.
Description: Series statement: Bo & Zop learn how to be an earthling |
   Originally published under title: Looking after your world: a book about the
   environment. King's Lynn: BookLife, 2020. | Includes index.
Identifiers: Canadiana (print) 20200225421 |
   Canadiana (ebook) 2020022543X |
   ISBN 9780778781202 (hardcover) |
   ISBN 9780778781240 (softcover) |
   ISBN 9781427125705 (HTML)
Subjects: LCSH: Environmental protection—Juvenile literature. |
   LCSH: Human ecology—Juvenile literature. | LCSH: Sustainable living—
   Juvenile literature. | LCSH: Conduct of life—Juvenile literature.
Classification: LCC GE195.5 .H65 2021 | DDC j363.7—dc23

Library of Congress Cataloging-in-Publication Data

Names: Holmes, Kirsty, author.
Title: How do earthlings look after their planet? / Kirsty Holmes.
Description: New York : Crabtree Publishing Company, 2021. |
   Series: Bo & Zop learn how to be an earthling | Includes index.
Identifiers: LCCN 2020016376 (print) | LCCN 2020016377 (ebook) |
   ISBN 9780778781202 (hardcover) |
   ISBN 9780778781240 (paperback) |
   ISBN 9781427125705 (ebook)
Subjects: LCSH: Environmentalism--Juvenile literature. | Environmental
   protection--Juvenile literature. | Human ecology--Juvenile literature.
Classification: LCC GE195.5 .H65 2021 (print) | LCC GE195.5 (ebook) |
   DDC 363.7--dc23
LC record available at https://lccn.loc.gov/2020016376
LC ebook record available at https://lccn.loc.gov/2020016377

Crabtree Publishing Company

www.crabtreebooks.com   1-800-387-7650

Published by Crabtree Publishing Company in 2021

©2020 BookLife Publishing Ltd

Printed in the U.S.A./072020/CG20200429

Published in Canada
Crabtree Publishing
616 Welland Avenue
St. Catharines, Ontario
L2M 5V6

Published in the United States
Crabtree Publishing
347 Fifth Ave
Suite 1402-145
New York, NY 10016

CONTENTS

Bo and Zop learn how to be an EARTHLING

Words with lines underneath, like <u>this</u>, can be found in the glossary on page 24.

SOMEWHERE IN THE SOLAR SYSTEM...

One star in the night sky is shining brighter than all the others. Can you see it? Is it really a star? Could it be a <u>satellite</u>? Or it could be... an alien spaceship!

Earth

Alien spaceship

Two brave aliens from planet Omegatron are on a mission to planet Earth. Their names are Bo and Zop. They want to learn all about <u>Earthlings</u> before they decide if Earth is safe to visit.

Bo and Zop are studying the <u>environment</u> on Earth. They are looking for a good place to land. They want to build a home there for all their friends from Omegatron.

The Amazon rain forest

"Zop, it's perfect! All we need to do is get rid of all those big green things."

"Do you mean the trees? That would be bad for Earth's environment, Bo!"

Bo thinks he has found a good place for a home. It has warm weather and plenty of room. But it is already home to a lot of trees and wildlife.

7

HOME SWEET HOME

There are different kinds of environments. Earth's environment is all the living and nonliving things on the planet that were not made by Earthlings.

"What is Earth's environment, Zop?"

Water

Weather

Air

Plants

Animals

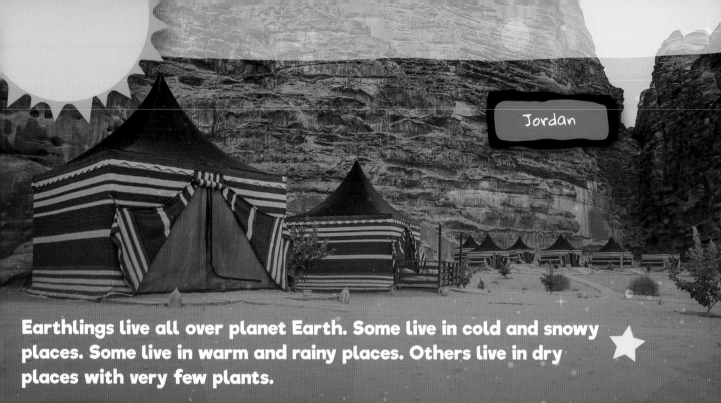

Jordan

Earthlings live all over planet Earth. Some live in cold and snowy places. Some live in warm and rainy places. Others live in dry places with very few plants.

Greenland

Hawaii, U.S.

9

EARTHLINGS NEED THE ENVIRONMENT

There are more than 7.5 billion Earthlings on planet Earth. They all depend on their environment. It gives them air to breathe, food to eat, warmth from the Sun, and water to drink.

Everything that Earthlings need can be found in the environment.

Earthlings also get many everyday <u>products</u> from Earth's environment. They get <u>fuel</u> such as oil from the ground. They get wood and paper from trees. They get <u>materials</u> for clothing from plants.

"Even though Earthlings live in houses and apartments, they still depend on Earth's environment."

EARTH IN TROUBLE

Earthlings use Earth's environment to get the things they need. But they sometimes harm it at the same time. These are some of the Earthling activities that damage the environment.

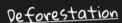

Pollution

Deforestation

Mining

PROTECTING THE ENVIRONMENT

Earthlings create a lot of garbage. That garbage can end up polluting land and water. It often harms the plants and animals that live there. Some animals, such as fish, could mistake garbage for food.

"Don't Earthlings need to drink water to live?"

"Yes, they do. Many of them eat fish too."

Earthlings work hard to solve the problem of pollution. They can try to create less garbage. One way to do this is to use fewer single-use plastics. These are plastic objects that are used just one time, then thrown away. They often end up in water.

Earthlings also work together to clean up pollution.

Trees are very important to life on Earth. They clean the air, help save water, and keep soil in place. But large areas of forest are often cut down for the wood or to make room for farms or homes. This is called deforestation.

"Deforestation causes animals to lose their homes. It also causes soil to wash away."

Many Earthlings help protect trees. They can use less paper. They can work together to plant new trees. They can speak out against deforestation.

These Earthlings plant new trees in their community.

One way Earthlings use less paper is to reuse paper scraps. Do you use scrap paper in your classroom?

Some Earthling activities pollute the air. Cars and factories burn <u>fossil fuels</u>, which give off gases that are not good for Earthlings. Other harmful gases can also be given off by farming and mining activities.

All Earthlings can play a part to help solve the problem of air pollution. They can choose not to use a car to get from place to place. They can choose to use or make products that do not give off harmful gases.

Some Earthlings ask companies to give off less air pollution.

Carpooling causes less air pollution. It means that fewer cars are on the road.

MAKING CHOICES

Earthlings can make everyday choices to help the environment. Choosing to reduce, reuse, and recycle is an important choice.

Recycling lets Earthlings turn old objects into materials that can be used again.

Composting food waste is one way Earthlings can create less waste.

Earthlings create less waste when they donate and reuse items such as clothing and toys.

Water power uses energy from flowing water.

Solar power uses the sun's energy.

Wind power uses wind energy.

"These ways to get energy do not cause air pollution."

"That's a great idea!"

Many Earthlings work very hard to come up with new ideas and solutions to help the environment. Some Earthlings created environmentally friendly ways to get <u>energy</u>.

BO AND ZOP'S NEW HOME

Earth is the only home they have, so all Earthlings need to take care of it. Bo and Zop need to build a home that does not harm the environment.

How would you plan a home that does not harm the environment?

- Where would you build it?
- What materials would you use?
- How would the home get energy?

Bo has learned a lot. He made a plan for an environmentally friendly home.

"That looks like a great place to live."

"We have to look after Earth's environment, Zop!"

GLOSSARY

composting Turning plant or food waste into a natural material

deforestation Cutting down large areas of forest

donate To give something away for a cause, such as charity

Earthlings Human beings

energy The power to do work

environment A person's surroundings

fossil fuels Fuels that formed from the remains of living things

fuel Material that is burned to create energy

materials Substances, such as wood or plastic, from which something can be made

mining Digging in the earth for certain materials

pollution Introducing waste into the environment, with harmful effects

products Items or substances made and sold by humans

satellite A human-made object that circles Earth or another space object

INDEX